S0-DQY-458

LIBERATING THE LIMERICK

230 Irresistible Classics

Edited by

ERNEST W. LEFEVER

Illustrated with fifteen *New Yorker* Cartoons

Hamilton Books
A member of
The Rowman & Littlefield Publishing Group
Lanham • Boulder • New York • Toronto • Oxford

Copyright © 2006 by
Hamilton Books
4501 Forbes Boulevard
Suite 200
Lanham, Maryland 20706
Hamilton Books Acquisitions Department (301) 459-3366

PO Box 317
Oxford
OX2 9RU, UK

All rights reserved
Printed in the United States of America
British Library Cataloging in Publication Information Available

Library of Congress Control Number: 2006921765
ISBN-13: 978-0-7618-3399-4 (paperback : alk. paper)
ISBN-10: 0-7618-3399-4 (paperback : alk. paper)

∞™ The paper used in this publication meets the minimum
requirements of American National Standard for Information
Sciences—Permanence of Paper for Printed Library Materials,
ANSI Z39.48—1984

For my Parents
Calvin Ashby Lefever (1881–1966)
and
Katie Roth Lefever (1885–1970)
Whose Quiet Humor and Commitment to Truth
Are Reflected in These Pages

CONTENTS

Introduction: The Enduring Limerick vii

Battle of the Sexes 1
Feminine Mystique 9
Religion and Philosophy 17
Padres and Preachers 23
History 28
Politics 32
Language and Literature 37
Music and the Arts 42
Science and Technology 48
Manners and Morals 56
Food and Drink 62
Freudian Quips 66
Death and Dying 72
Celebrities 77
Man and Beast 80
Sheer Nonsense 89

Sources and Credits 99
Index of Authors 101
About the Author 105

INTRODUCTION . . .
THE ENDURING LIMERICK

The limerick, a quintessentially English literary form, was born in Victorian Britain and has flourished ever since in the halls of academe and beyond. The widely held myth that the limerick is hog tied to the seamier side of the human drama persists. True, the great majority of published verses have been vulgar, rude, or scatological, albeit funny. As the American linguist, Morris Bishop, once put it:

> The limerick is furtive and mean;
> You must keep her in close quarantine
> Or she sneaks to the slum
> And promptly becomes
> Disorderly, drunk, or obscene.

And an anonymous writer added:

> Most limericks are callous and crude.
> Their morals are frequently lewd.
> They are not worth reading
> By persons of breeding.
> They're designed for the vulgar and rude.

This collection of 230 verses by fifty authors, past and present, demonstrates that limericks can be wise, hilarious, and often sexy without being obscene. The writers address the whole range of human experience—from psychology and politics, to science and religion, to culture and the arts—with more than a little humor and wisdom crammed into five disciplined lines.

Though crude and lewd verses have been banished, the limericks in this book lay bare the foibles of the human drama with wit and irony. Many reflect the persistence of sex, raw ambition, and the drive for recognition in everyday life. Timorously, I have assigned the verses to categories, such as Battle of the Sexes, Feminine Mystique, Freudian Quips, Padres and Preachers, as well as History, Politics, and Literature.

The notable literary figures included here—Sir. William S. Gilbert, Robert Louis Stevenson, Oliver Wendell Holmes, Archbishop William Temple, W. H. Auden, Bertrand Russell, and Ogden Nash—demonstrate that limericks can be wise and whimsical. They can be savored by a machine politicians, *New Yorker* readers, and your maiden aunt in Dubuque.

Assembling this collection was an arduous task. I read or scanned more than 9,000 limericks in two dozen books. The great majority of these verses were prurient or scatological. There were numerous duplications and many were anonymous. The origin of others was impossible to trace.

The lure and lore of the limerick go back to Edward Lear (1812–1888), the man in the runcible hat whose nonsense verses and drawings have amused children of all ages ever since. As a child, I ran about the house reciting Lear's verses and composed some of my own.

Unlike the world's shortest poem—*Fleas:* Adam Had 'em—the limerick has an established form. It may be defined as a verse of five lines. The first, second, and fifth lines rhyme and usually have eight or nine syllables. The third and fourth also rhyme and generally have five or six syllables. Like other limerick lovers, I readily acknowledge that these verses do not qualify as poetry.

Many limerick writers indulge in word play and other literary devices to capture the fantasy and imagination of the reader. However written, the good ones appeal to a wide range of passions and convictions. A near contemporary of Lear, U.S. Supreme Court Justice, Oliver Wendell Holmes, Sr. (1809–1894), wrote several enduring limericks, including this classic that embraces the subtle word play found in the best verses:

> Said the Reverend Henry Ward Beecher
> "The hen is an elegant creature."
> The hen pleased with that
> Laid an egg in his hat—
> And thus did the hen reward Beecher

Strange perhaps, but I could find only a few American literary figures who have written notable limericks, Ogden Nash being the chief exception.

The verses in this volume embrace a wide range of characters from Adam, Eve, Noah, Moses, and Sampson to Washington, William H. Taft, Gerald Ford, and Al Sharpton. The ancients include Saint Augustine, Socrates, Archimedes, and Oedipus Rex. Between then and the modern era, Luther, Calvin, Shakespeare (clothed), and Lady Godiva make their appearance.

Then, tumbling over one another are such characters as Bach, Strauss, Kant, Machiavelli, Darwin, Goya, and Gauguin.

Closer to our time are Gandhi, Bernard Shaw, Freud, Einstein, Albert Camus, Reinhold Niebuhr, Henry Ford, Herman Kahn, and Cecil B. DeMille.

Why should I, author of a dozen books on ethics and politics, stoop to compiling a book on limericks? Frankly, I don't regard this collection as a descent. Many, perhaps most, of these verses reflect facets of truth and virtue wrapped in the garments of irony and caricature.

In this effort, I had the good-humored advice of friends—-including a theologian, a physician, a broker, and a clinical psychologist. I want to thank my two sons, David and Bryce, a nephew, Timothy Lefever, and my brother John David. Also Patricia Buckley Bozell and Robert Gessert.

While avoiding the abyss of lurid sex or pornography, this collection includes old classics, as well as more recently published verses and a few unsteady ones by the editor. I have made strenuous efforts to get permission from published authors.

Each section is introduced by a cartoon from The New Yorker, for which permission has been granted. (See Note on Sources and Credits before the Index of Authors.)

Some of the limericks included here have been slightly modified by the editor for reasons of clarity or meter; they are indicated by an asterisk (*)

Read, enjoy, and write some verses of your own.

—Ernest W. Lefever

Chevy Chase, Maryland
Christmas 2005

BATTLE OF THE SEXES

SIPRESS

"I'm not yelling at you, I'm yelling with you."
—New Yorker, Feb. 19 and 26, 2001

1

1

A cute secretary, none cuter,
Was replaced by a clicking computer;
   'Twas the wife of the boss
   Put this deal across,
You see, the computer was neuter.

—Ogden Nash

2

There was an old fellow of Lyme,
Who lived with three wives at a time.
   When asked, "Why the third?"
   He replied, "One's absurd,
"And bigamy, sir, is a crime!"

—Cosmo Monkhouse

3

She hadn't on even a slip
Between her tight dress and her hip.
   She said, "I forgot."
   He said, "You did not.
"You are wearing a Freudian slip.

—Laurence Perrine

4

Though Godiva knew she'd be fined,
She had fully made up her mind.
  On her steed she streaked,
  And nobody peeked,
Except Little Tom, who went blind.
  —Harry Thomas*

5

Wanting children, a couple once sat
For a course on how to begat,
  When the doctor expounded,
  They stood up dumb founded,
And said they could never do *that*.
  —G. W. Hanney

6

A prolific mother named Hall
Who seemed to have triplets each Fall,
  When asked why and wherefore,
  Said, "That's what we're here for,
" But we often get nothing at all."
  —anon

7

Despite her impressive physique
Lolita was really quite meek.
  If a mouse showed its head
  She would jump into bed
With an awful blood-curdling sheik.

                —anon

8

A lissome neurotic named Jane
Once kissed every man on a train.
  Said she, "Please don't panic,
  "I'm just nymphomaniac—
"'Twould be more fun were I sane."

                —anon

9

There once was a maid with such graces
That her curves cried out for embraces,
  "You look," said McGee,
  "Like a million to me—
Invested in *all* the right places.

                —anon

10

Said an ovum one night to a sperm,
"You're a very attractive young germ!
    Come join me, my sweet,
    Let our nuclei meet
In nine months we'll both come to term.

—anon

11

There was a sultan named Darrem
Who liked to play tricks on his harem.
    He caught him a mouse
    Which he loosed in the house
And he called the result-—"harum-scarum!"

—anon

12

A Turk named Abdulla Ben Barum
Had sixty-five wives in his harem.
    When his favorite horse died,
    "Mighty Allah!" he cried.
"Take a few of my wives—I can spare 'em."

—anon

13

A round-the-world traveler named Anne
Took up with a Tokyo man.
   The relationship thrived
   And her baby arrived
With its bottom stamped "Made in Japan."

—anon

14

A charming young lady named Rood,
Was more than a bit of a prude.
   She pulled down the blind
   When changing her mind,
Lest an evil eye should intrude.

—anon

15

One day when a lady named Anne
Went up on the sunroof to tan,
   A guy in a 'copter
   Flew over and dropped her
Some ads for a crash-diet plan.

—John Ciardi

16

The nudists, by pure thoughts possessed,
Were gathered for prayer before rest,
   But one wanton boy
   Eyed his ravishing Joy
And dreamt how she'd look fully dressed.
—Laurence Perrine

17

A bather whose garments were strewed
On the beach where she bathed all nude,
   Saw a man come along
   —And unless I'm quite wrong,
You expected this line to be lewd.
—anon*

18

A straight-laced warrior of Parma,
Lovingly caressed his charmer.
   Said the maiden demure,
   "You'll excuse me, I'm sure,
But I wish you'd take off your armor."
—anon

19

There was a young person named Clarence,
Who cabled from Sweden: "Dear Parents:
  "Sex-change operation
  "Creates new relation.
"As Clara, implore your forbearance."

—John Ciardi

FEMININE MYSTIQUE

"You've made me very happy, Ted, but now I want to be miserable again."
—New Yorker, July 30, 2001

20

There was a young lady from Wilts,
　　Who walked up to Scotland on stilts.
　　　　When they said it was shocking
　　　　To show so much stocking,
　　She answered, "Then what about kilts?"

—Edward Lear

21

"Will you join the Animal Fair?
　　All the birds and beasts will be there,"
　　　　Said Adam to his madam.
　　　　Eve replied, "But Adam
　　"I haven't a thing to wear."

—Laurence Perrine*

22

There was a young girl named Bianca
Who retired while the ship was at anchor;
　　　　But awoke, with dismay,
　　　　When she heard the mate say:
"We must pull up the top sheet and spanker."

—anon

23

A crusader's wife slipped from the garrison
For a quiet affair with a Saracen;
 She was not over-sexed,
 Or jealous or vexed,
She just wanted to make a comparison.

      —Ogden Nash

24

A frisky young lady of Florence,
For kissing professed great abhorrence,
 When first she'd been kissed.
 And found what she'd missed,
She cried till the tears came in torrents.

      —anon

25

A publisher went off to France,
In search for a tale of romance;
 But a Parisian lady
 Told a story so shady
That the publisher made an advance.

      —anon

26

A sprightly young lass of Lynn
Was deep in original sin.
  When they urged, "Do be good!"
  She said, "Would if I could!"
And straightaway went at it again.

—anon

27

There was a young lady of Kent
Who said she knew what it meant
  When men asked her to dine,
  And served cocktails and wine;
She knew what it meant, but she went.

—anon

28

There was a young lady named Ruth,
Who had a great passion for truth.
  She said she would die
  Before she would lie.
And she died in the prime of her youth.

—anon

29

A lithe young maid of Ostend,
Swore she'd hold out to the end;
   Alas, half-way over,
   'Twixt Calais and Dover,
She did what she didn't intend.

                    —anon*

30

I once knew a spinster of Staines,
And a spinster that lady remains;
   She's no figure nor looks
   Neither dances nor cooks—
And most ghastly of all, she has brains.

                    —anon

31

A study that tears me apart
Says that breast-fed babies are smart.
   That fact that I'm dumb
   Isn't my fault, chum.
I was bottle-fed from the start.

                 —Lyn Nofziger*

32

As a beauty, I'm not a great star,
There are others more handsome by far;
    But my face, I don't mind it,
    Because I'm behind it,
It's the folks in front that I jar.

                          —Anthony Euwer

33

A young girl who was no good at tennis
And at swimming was really a menace,
    Took pains to explain:
    "It depends how you train:
"I was a street-walker in Venice."

                          —anon

34

There was a young lady of Pecking
Who indulged in a great deal of necking;
    This seemed a great waste
    Since she claimed to be chaste;
This statement, however, needs checking.

                          —anon*

35

There was a young lady named Wylde
Who kept herself quite undefiled
   By thinking of Jesus,
   Contagious diseases,
And the bother of having a child.

             —anon

36

A rosy-cheeked lass from Dunellen.
Whom the Hoboken sailors called Helen,
   In her efforts to please
   Has spread social disease
From New York to the Straits of Magellan.

             —anon

37

There was a young lady from Thrace
Whose corsets grew too tight to lace.
   Her mother said, "Nelly,
   "There's more in your belly
Than ever went in through your face."

             —anon

38

A blunt speaking lady in Kent,
Always said just what she meant;
   People said, "She's a dear,
   "So unique, so sincere—"
But they shunned her by common consent.

              —anon

39

A lawyer with a high IQ
Was wed to a two-timing shrew.
   When he complained
   "Shut up," she explained
And out of the bedroom he flew

          —Ernest Lefever

40

An authoress, living in Trim,
Possessed a remarkable whim.
   She wore a blue bonnet
   When writing a sonnet;
A helmet when writing a hymn.

            —anon

RELIGION AND PHILOSOPHY

"Theologian? You guys are always fun."
—New Yorker, Dec. 20 & 27, 2004

41

God's plan made a hopeful beginning
But man spoiled his chances by sinning.
  We trust that the story
  Will end in God's glory;
But, at present, the other side's winning.
          —Oliver Wendell Holmes

42

Our God, some contend, is immutable,
Their faith is, indeed, irrefutable:
  When He does what He should,
  It's because He is Good.
When he doesn't, He is inscrutable.
          —Laurence Perrine

43

On one point, and one point alone,
Concerning the known and unknown,
  All religions agree:
  "All creeds that may be.
"Are in error excepting our own."
          —Laurence Perrine

44

Saint Augustine thought he had found
The sin by which mankind is bound:
   "It was not," so said he,
   "The fruit on the tree,
But the lust of the pair on the ground."
             —Bob L. Staples

45

The indulgence sales vexed Luther sore,
And he angrily screamed and he swore:
   "By writing 95 theses,
   "I'll tear Rome to pieces!
"And nail them to the Wittenberg Door."
             —Bob L. Staples*

46

At Oxford when Niebuhr had quitted
Said a bright student, "I have hit it.
   "Since I cannot do right,
   "I will go out tonight
"Find the best sin to commit and commit it."
           —Archbishop William Temple*

47

The Devil, who plays a large part,
Has tricked his way into your heart
    By simple insistence
    On his non-existence—
Which really is devilish smart.

—anon

48

There once was a man who said, "God
"Must think it exceedingly odd
    "If he finds that this tree
    "Continues to be,
"When there's no one about in the Quad."

—Ronald Knox

49

Dear Sir, Your astonishment's odd;
I am always about in the Quad.
    And that's why the tree
    Will continue to be,
Since seen by Yours faithfully, God.

—anon

50

This very young student named Fred,
When questioned on Descartes, he said:
 "It is perfectly clear
 "That I'm not really here,
"For I haven't a thought in my head."
     —V. R. Romero*

51

Without being oratorical,
Consider Kant's categorical
 Should one treat one's friends
 As means or as ends?
Or is the query rhetorical?
     —Ernest Lefever

52

A Calvinist preacher said "Damn!
"I'm wholly convinced that I am
 "An engine that moves
 "In predestined grooves:
"I'm not even a bus, but a tram."
     —M. E. Hare*

53

Moses prayed, when he saw the Red Sea,
"Lord. have You some guidance for me?"
    God said, "Read Instructions
    "For Meeting Obstructions,
"Look under 'DeMille, Cecil B.'"

—Bob L. Staples

54

A clergyman read from his text
How Samson was sissored and vexed,
    Then a barber arose
    From his Sunday morn doze,
Was rattled, and shouted, "Who's next?"

—anon

55

"Of geeks, nerds, and quacks I'll have none,"
Said God when his work had begun.
    "CIA men will do
    "When I'm caught in a stew,
"But theologians are the most fun."

—Ernest Lefever

PADRES AND PREACHERS

"Do you think of yourself as a spiritual person?"
—New Yorker, Oct. 22, 2001

56

An assistant professor named Dodd
Had manners arresting and odd.
    He said, "If you please,
    "Spell my name with three d's,
"Though one is sufficient for God."

—anon*

57

A Boston Cardinal named Law
Had an unforgivable flaw.
    He greeted pedophiles
    With winks and with smiles,
Instead of a sock on the jaw.

—Lyn Nofziger*

58

There was a young monk of Siberia,
Who of fasting grew wearier and wearier,
    Till at length, with a yell,
    He burst forth from his cell,
And devoured the Mother Superior.

—anon*

59

Said a naughty madam named Belle,
Whom her preacher threatened with Hell,
   "I have no regrets,
   "No doubts, and no debts,
"If I haven't done good, I've done well."

                     —anon

60

A minister up in Vermont
Keeps a goldfish alive in the font;
   When he dips the babes in
   It tickles their skin,
Which is all the innocents want.

                     —anon

61

There once was a pious young priest
Who lived almost wholly on yeast;
   "For," he said, "it is plain
   "We must all rise again,"
And I want to get started at least.

                     —anon

62

Said a practical thinker: "One should
"Help to slay superstition for good.
  "I, for instance, refuse
  "To observe all taboos,
"With immunity, so far, touch wood."

—Frank Watson

63

There was a faith-healer from Deal
Who said: "Though my pain isn't real,
  "If I sit on a pin,
  "And it punctures my skin,
"I dislike what I fancy I feel."

—anon

64

Oh, my name is John Wellington Wells,
I'm a dealer in magic and spells,
  In blessings and curses
  And ever-filled purses,
In prophecies, witches, and knells.

—W. S. Gilbert

65

Rev. Sharpton is a public clown.
Rev. Jackson wears his phony frown.
  Both keep belting their song
  But their grammar is wrong.
Rev's an adjective, not a noun.

              —Ernest Lefever

HISTORY

"Just look at you! How many ex-dictators can still fit into their dictator suits?"
—New Yorker, June 11, 2001

66

Yelled a Communist, "Down with the Pope,
"And all the crowned heads of Eu-rope!
  "Equal rights is our creed.
  "What more do we need?"
And someone shouted out—"Soap!"

—anon

67

Said a Marxist who stood on a pier:,
"You may regard my views rather queer,
  "I could gambol all day
  "With the sharks in the bay,
"It's the ones in striped pants that I fear."

—W. H. G. Price*

68

How grim is the socialist plan
To create a new Marxist Man
  Who'll be malleably meek
  And in no way unique
In a world that is hopelessly bland.

—F. R. Duplantier*

69

The prized Grecian urn was quite rare—
Wholly owned by one millionaire—
    When the Red Guards
    Smashed it to shards
Every comrade got his fair share.

              —Laurence Perrine*

70

There was a bland sage of New Delhi,
Who said: "When you're kicked in the belly,
    "By a neighboring tribe,
    "Don't browbeat or bribe—
"Be Gandhi, and not Machiavelli."

              —Joyce Parr*

71

Said Wellington: "What is the location
Of this battle I've won for the nation?"
    They replied: "Waterloo."
    He said: "That will do.
"What a glorious name for a station!"

              —Frank Richards*

72

A Tory, once out in his motor,
Ran over a Laborite voter.
   "Thank goodness," he cried,
   "He was on the wrong side,
"I don't blame myself one iota."

            —A. W. Webster

73

George Washington told the brigade
On the Delaware, "I'm afraid.
   "Since the advantage here lies
   "In total surprise,
"The decision is *row v. wade.*"

            —A. N. Wilkins*

74

Noah's sons thought the old man was manic,
His work ethic had caused them to panic.
   He fed them on oats
   Like donkeys and goats,
But at least they weren't on the *Titanic!*

            —Rob L. Staples*

POLITICS

"Sure, meritocracies are fine, but why take the chance?"
—New Yorker, June 13 & 20, 2005

75

God brought the first man to fruition,
But viewing the scraps with contrition,
    He collected the junk,
    And created the skunk,
The snake, and the first politician.

—Douglas Catley

76

What have you done said Christine,**
You ruined the Party machine
    To lie in the nude
    Is not at all rude,
But to lie in the House is obscene!"

—anon

77

The CBS newsman Cronkite
Claimed ten m1llion viewers each night.
    He slanted the news
    To fit his own views.
He knew in "his heart he was right."

—Ernest Lefever

**In 1963, a British Minister lied to Commons about his affair with party girl Christine Keeler who was also involved with a Soviet naval attaché.

78

In the days of mild Jerry Ford,
Decorum and calm were restored;
 He did nothing hateful,
 For which we were grateful,
And terribly, terribly bored.

      —anon

79

Historians and linguists may miss
The apposite nature of this,
 But the sound that a snake
 Is given to make
Was a surname well suited to Hiss.

     —F. R. Duplantier

80

There is no reason, nor rhyme
To what we hear all the time,
 And the "facts" they rehearse
 Are often the reverse,
Like: "Poverty causes crime!"

     —F. R. Duplantier*

81

Adding Euro- or Afro- won't do:
Ethnic conflict will only ensue.
   No hyphen for me:
   I'm happy to be
An American—through and through.
            —F. R. Duplantier

82

Here's an end to the race-baiting game
And the constant assignment of blame:
   We'll talk about race
   Till we're blue in the face,
Then we'll all look exactly the same!
            —F. R. Duplantier

83

"This case was a good one for me,"
Said a lawyer, collecting his fee.
   "The victim got stung,
   "The jury was hung,
"And the criminal got off scot-free."
            —Laurence Perrine

84

When spreading the deadly anthrax
Without leaving a trace of your tracks
    You can send it by mail,
    But you are bound to fail
If you try to spread it by FAX.

—Lyn Nofziger

LANGUAGE AND LITERATURE

"By the way, does anything other than 'trouble' rhyme with 'bubble'?"
—New Yorker, Nov. 1, 2004

85

A novelist of the Absurd
Has a voice that will shortly be heard;
 I learn from my spies
 He's about to devise
An unprintable three-letter word.

       —Ogden Nash

86

Thirteen amateur players, most brave,
A performance of *Hamlet* once gave.
 Said a wag, "Now let's see
 If it's Bacon or he—
That is, Shakespeare—who turned in his grave!"

         —anon*

87

Did Ophelia ask Hamlet to bed?
Was Gertrude incestuously wed?
 There is one thing that's certain,
 By the fall of the curtain,
Almost everyone's certainly dead.

        —A. Cinna*

88

Poor Ophelia sighed, "I deplore
"The fact that young Hamlet's a bore.
 "He just talks to himself;
 "I'll be left on the shelf,
"Or go mad by the end of Act IV."
—Frank Richards

89

An old Danish jester named Yorick
Drank a gallon of paregoric;
 "My jokes have been dull,"
 He said, "but my skull
"Will one of these days be historic."
—Ogden Nash

90

Desdemona by Othello was choked.
When he learned she was guiltless, he joked,
 "Oh, what sad twisted ends,
 "When you can't trust your friends!"
He then fell on his dagger and croaked.
—Anatole T. Lubovich*

91

The Marquis de Sade and Genet
Are most highly thought of today;
   But torture and treachery
   Are not my sort of lechery,
So I've given my copies away.

          —W. H. Auden

92

There was a young man of Moose Jaw
Who wanted to see Bernard Shaw;
   When they asked him why,
   He made no reply,
But sharpened his ax and a saw.

          —*Punch*, 1918

93

There was a young poet from Kew,
Who failed to emerge into view,
   So he said, "I'll dispense
   "With rhyme, meter, and sense,"
He did, and he's now in *Who's Who*.

          —anon

94

There was an old puzzler, Ben Ross,
Who died—doing crosswords, of course
   He was buried, poor Ben,
   With eraser and pen
In a box six feet down, three across.

—Sheila Anne Barry

95

Once a sturdy African Mau-Mau
Got into an extended row-row.
   The cause of the friction?
   When practicing diction,
Saying: "How-how now-now brown-brown cow-cow?"

—anon*

96

A third grader who lives in Bucyrus
Has unleashed a computerized virus
   That endangers us all,
   In large countries and small,
Excepting those still using papyrus.

—Maynard Kaplan*

MUSIC AND THE ARTS

"Maybe someday we could set aside a cave just for art"
—New Yorker, July 16, 2001

97

A tone-deaf old person of Tring,
When somebody asked him to sing.
   Replied, "It's a bit odd,
    "But I can never tell *God*
"*Save the Weasel* from *Pop Goes the King*."
                —anon*

98

I'm so very talented and smart,
But who, oh who, will give me a start?
   So I'll rev up a chant
   For an NEA grant
To finance my career in fine art.
            —F. R. Duplantier*

99

A mordant and decadent youth
Said, "Beauty is greater than truth.
   "But by beauty I mean
   "The obscure, the obscene
"The diseased, decayed, and uncouth."
          —Thomas Thorneley*

100

A painter, his canvas still wet,
Said, "No, we are not finished yet.
  "When you pose in the nude
  "There's a short interlude
"While we wait for the paint to set."

—Laurence Perrine*

101

Said the Duchess of Alba to Goya:
"Paint some pictures to hang in my foya!"
  So he painted her twice:
  In the nude to look nice,
And then in her clothes, to annoya.

—anon

102

"Monsieur Gauguin? 'E's gone to Tahiti,
"Where ze girls are so friendly and pretty;
  "'E paints them *tout* bare,
  "'Wiz zair lovely black 'air
"And bodies zo—'ow you say 'meaty'!"

—Stanley J. Sharpless

103

A Victorian gent said: "This dance
"The can-can that we've got from France,
   "Fills me with disgust—
   "It generates lust—
"But see it while you have the chance."
              —Frank Richards*

104

A poor painter unburdened by cash,
Said: "It's time to be making a splash.
   "I can paint, if I care,
   "Things to startle and scare,
"Though I'm fully aware they're trash."
              —Thomas Thorneley*

105

Our music is technically slack,
Inharmonious, noisy, and black.
   Its ear-splitting strain
   Evokes the "Refrain!
Oh, Johann Sebastian come Bach!"
              —Laurence Perrine*

106

The fabulous Wizard of Oz
Retired from his business becoz
    What with up-to-date science
    To most of his clients,
He wasn't the Wizard he woz.

—anon*

107

There was a trombonist called Herb,
Whose playing was loud, though superb;
    When neighbors complained,
    Young Herbert explained:
"But great art is meant to disturb!"

—Ron Rubin

108

A tutor who taught on the flute
Tried to teach two young tooters to toot.
    Asked the two to the tutor,
    "Is it harder to toot, or
"To tutor two tooters to toot?"

—Carolyn Wells

109

Some charming sections from Strauss
Were boisterously played at our house;
   We shouted "Encore!"
   And clamored for more.
The neighbors did nothing but grouse.

—anon*

110

To compose a sonata today,
Don't proceed in the old-fashioned way;
   Take a seat on the keys,
   Bump about as you please.
"Oh how modern!" the critics will say.

—anon

111

Suddenly the great prima donna
Cried, "Gawd, but my voice is a goner!"
   But a cat in the wings
   Said, "I know how she sings,"
And finished her solo with honor.

—anon*

SCIENCE AND TECHNOLOGY

"And this light here lets you know when the camera is obsolete."
—New Yorker, Feb. 28, 2005

112

Said a chimp as he swung by his tale
To his offspring, both female and male:
   "Don't worry my dears,
   "In a few thousand years,
"You'll be teaching the students at Yale!"

      —anon

113

A monkey sprang down from a tree
And vigorously cursed Charles D.
   "I hold with the Bible,"
   He cried. "It's a libel
"That man is descended from me!"

      —Laurence Perrine

114

A fragile fellow named Bryan,
Was always cryin' and cryin'.
   "Do you think that my shape
   "Was derived from an ape?
"I know that Darwin was lyin'."

      —Berton Braley*

115

Archimedes, an early truth-seeker.
Lept out of his bath, cried "Eureka!"
   And ran half a mile,
   Wearing only a smile,
Thus becoming the very first streaker.
              —Stanley J. Sharpless

116

Herman Kahn the big thinker once said,
"I don't want to be Red *or* be dead,
   "Lets think the unthinkable
   "And war-game the brinkable
"So we end up with peace *and* with bread."
              —Ernest Lefever

117

After swallowing radium, Miss Errant
Said, explaining her deed so aberrant,
   "If approached in the park.
   "Now, I'll glow in the dark,
For I'm armed with a nuclear deterrent!"
              —Vasser W. Smith

118

I played chess with my robot at 10:00,
And he rapidly took all my men.
　　When I played him at 2:00.
　　I'd adjusted a screw,
And now *I'm* the master again.
　　　　　　　　　—Laurence Perrine

119

Wee Jamie, a canny young Scot,
Observed, when a kettle was hot,
　　That steam raised the lid,
　　And thanks to this kid,
Now everyone knows Watt's watt.
　　　　　　　　　—Joyce Johnson*

120

"What this country needs," Henry roared.
"Is not a new Rolls or a Chord,
　　"But a factory clone
　　"That a poor man can own,
"And that you and I can—a Ford!"
　　　　　　　　　—Laurence Perrine

121

Mine is a very unusual case:
I was wed way out in cyberspace,
   My spouse and I met
   By chance on the 'Net,
But we haven't yet met face to face.

           —F. R. Duplantier*

122

Two brothers devised what a sight—
A bicycle crossed with a kite.
   They predicted—rash pair!
   It would fly through the air!
And what do you know. They were Wright!

           —Laurence Perrine*

123

There was an old fellow at Trinity
Who solved the square root of Infinity.
   But it gave him such fidgets
   To count up the digits
He chucked Math and took up Divinity.

           —anon*

124

An intriguing young woman named Bright
Said she could travel faster than light.
   She set out one day,
   In a relative way,
And she returned the previous night.

—A. H. R. Buller

125

Said a pupil of Einstein, "It's rotten
"To find that I'd completely forgotten
   "That by living so fast
   "All my future is my past,
"And I'm buried before I'm begotten."

—C. F. Best*

126

A dozen, a gross, and a score,
Plus three times the square root of four,
   Divided by seven
   Plus five times eleven
Equals nine squared plus zero, no more.

—anon

127

A computer, to print out a fact
Will divide, multiply, and subtract.
 But the output can be
 No more than debris
If the input was less than exact.

       —anon*

128

The mosquito was heard to complain
That a chemist had poisoned his brain;
 The cause of his sorrow
 Was Paradichloro-
Diphenyltrichlorothane.

       —anon

129

He mastered Greek logic in Spain.
And conquered geometry—plain.
 With his mind at full throttle
 He can best Aristotle.
I wish I could download his brain.

       —Ernest Lefever

130

A suave ameba and his brother,
Were having a drink with each other.
In the midst of their quaffing
They split themselves laughing,
And each of them now is a mother.

—anon

MANNERS AND MORALS

"As a mitigating circumstance, may I say that my client's getaway car was a hybrid."
—New Yorker, Aug. 8 & 15, 2005

131

Said a right wealthy Texan in Rome,
Who had just purchased St. Peter's dome,
   "It's not just for the art,
   "Though I'd say that's right smart,
"It's the challenge of getting it home."

—John Ciardi*

132

I love all trees and buzzing bees
And great things like the Seven Seas.
   Everything global
   Makes me feel noble
But I still have a problem with fleas.

—Ernest Lefever

133

'Tis strange how the newspapers honor
A person who's called prima donna.
   They say not a thing
   Of how she can sing
But reams on the clothes she has on her.

—Eugene Field

134

A chic young sculptor named Phidias
Had a distaste for the hideous;
   So he sculpt Aphrodite
   Without any nightie,
Which shocked the ultra-fastidious.

—anon

135

There's a singer in Long Island City
Whose form is impressively pretty;
   She is often addressed
   By the name of "Beau Chest,"
Which is thought to be tasteful and witty.

—anon

136

Cried a slender young lady named Tony
With a bottom exceedingly bony,
   "I'll say this for my rump:
   "Though it may not be plump,
"It's my own and not a silicone phony!"

—anon

137

A popular composer named Bong
Tossed together a new with-it song.
   It was simply the croon
   Of a lovesick baboon,
With occasional thumps on the gong,
           —anon*

138

The teacher now has a new ploy
For youngsters who tend to annoy:
   For fussin' and fidgetin',
   Prescribe them some Ritalin
And cure them from being a boy!
         —F. R. Duplantier*

139

If you want to be part of the team,
You will have to abide by our theme:
   Kids don't really need
   To learn, reckon, or read
As long as they have self-esteem.
         —F. R. Duplantier*

140

At my junior high no one cares
About violence, drugs, and affairs.
  Bur a teacher's on hand
  With a swift reprimand
When a student is caught saying prayers.
  —F. R. Duplantier

141

Can anyone living recall
One person with ego so small
  That he'd given up smoking
  Without than invoking
Any notice from others *at all?*
  —Laurence Perrine

142

Here's a survey that needs to be done
On the merits of owning a gun.
  Ask anyone harmed
  By a thug who was armed
If he wishes he, too, had had one.
  —F. R. Duplantier

143

Said a very erudite ermine,
"There's one thing I cannot determine;
    "When a miss wears my coat
    "She's a person of note
"While I am a species of vermin!"

—anon*

FOOD AND DRINK

"*And do you take your organic green tea with sugar, lemon, honey, or just the usual dollop of smug self-righteousness?*"

—New Yorker, April 11, 2005

144

There was a young wife who beg·
Three husky boys— Nat, Pat, anu _
  When they all yelled for food,
  A big problem ensued
She found there was no tit for Tat.

—anon*

145

An epicure, dining at Crewe,
Found quite a large mouse in his stew.
  Said the waiter, "Don't shout,
  "And wave it about,
"Or the rest will be wanting one too!"

—anon

146

An oyster from old Timbuktu,
Confessed he was feeling quite blue.
  "For," said he, "as a rule,
  "When the weather turns cool,
"I'm apt to get into a stew."

—anon*

147

A pretty young girl from Mobile,
Went up in a large Ferris wheel.
    When halfway around,
    She glanced at the ground.
It cost her a ten-dollar meal.

                   —anon*

148

A glutton who hailed from the Rhine
When asked at what hour he would dine.
    He replied, "At eleven,
    "And at three, five, and seven,
"And eight and a quarter past nine."

                   —anon*

149

There was a young girl named Anheuser
Who said that no man could surprise her.
    But Old Overholt
    Gave her virtue a jolt,
And now she is sadder Budweiser.

                   —anon

150

A man whose illness was chronic,
When told he needed a tonic,
    Said, "Oh! Doctor dear,
    "Please make it a beer?"
"Nein," warned the Doc, "that Teutonic.

—anon*

151

What a flaw in your make-up and mine
When we go out to shop or to dine
    Makes an item appear
    At $5 too dear,
But a bargain at $4.99?

—Lurence Perrine

FREUDIAN QUIPS

"Tell me about your mother again, this time in a slow, sultry falsetto."
—New Yorker, June 6, 2005

152

The famous psychiatrist Freud
Of ethics was wholly devoid.
  When feeding his Id
  He did what he did
Leaving a large vacuous void.

               —Ernest Lefever

153

Said Freud: "I've discovered the Id.
"Of all your repressions be rid.
  "It won't ease the gravity
  "Of total depravity,
"But you'll know why you did what you did."

               —Frank Richards

154

"I did what I did," declared Id.
"I wish you had hid what you did,"
  Said Ego. "Amigo,
  "-Proclaimed Superego,
"But we shouldn't have done what you did."

               —Laurence Perrine*

155

In Vienna, the bastion of Freud!
Where bright surgeons are always employed;
    The boys with soft hands
    Are given new glands
And the two-fisted girls are de-boyed.

              —anon*

156

The Honorable Winifred Weems
Saw snails and snakes in her dreams,
    And these she enjoyed
    Until she heard Freud
Say: "Nothing is quite like it seems."

              —anon*

157

Said Sophocles, while putting his X
On the contract for "Oedipus Rex,"
    "I know it will run
    "Until the Year One,
"If the producer plays up the sex."

              —John Ciardi*

158

Said old Socrates, keeping his poise,
"Tell Xanthippe I've done with her noise.
   If she asks what you mean,
   Just say, when last seen
I was drinking with some of the boys."
                   —John Ciardi*

159

The Homeric young fighter Achilles
Was great with the fair Trojan fillies,
   "But," said Paris, "we'll
   "Just aim at his heel."
Now Achilles is pushing up lilies.
                   —Isaac Asimov

160

Said Tiresias to Oedipus Rex,
"I'm too old to care about sex,
   But I'm telling you, brother.
   That queen's a mean mother
And she's setting you up for a hex.
                   —John Ciardi

161

Old Oedipus said to the Sphinx:
"My name's been perverted by shrinks.
   "For a hefty price,
   "They say I'm not nice,
"I think that psychiatry stinks."

—Victor Gray*

162

A psychiatrist fellow from Rye
Went to visit another close by,
   Who said with a grin
   As he welcomed him in:
"Hullo, Smith! You're all right! How am I?"

—Stephen Cass

163

Though your dreams may seem normal and right,
They bring horrible things to the light;
   You can only be sure
   That you're perfectly pure
If you dream about nothing all—all night.

—anon.

164

For ten years I was humble, till when
I saw myself the humblest of men,
    That filled me with pride
    I burst, and near died.
Now I'm proud to be humble again.

—Laurence Perrine*

165

A young schizophrenic Struther,
When told of the death of his brother,
    Said, "Oh yes it's too bad,
    "But I can't feel that sad—
"After all, I still have each other."

—anon*

166

There was a young girl of Shanghai.
Who was so exceedingly shy,
    That undressing at night
    She turned out the light
For fear of the All-Seeing Eye.

—Bertrand Russell

DEATH AND DYING

"Dear, there's someone here to collect your soul."
—New Yorker, Nov. 1, 2004

167

The black Styx-born ferry to Hades,
Is for newly dead men and ladies.
    All are welcomed the same,
    Howsoever they came,
Whether by foot, beast, or Mercedes.
               —J. Maynard Kaplan*

168

"To Necropolis, City of Death,"
A classical philosopher saith,
    "All reluctantly go;
    "Yet no matter how slow,
"On arrival, they're all out of breath."
              —Laurence Perrine*

169

There was an old man who averred
He had learned to fly like a bird;
    Cheered by thousands of people
    He leapt from the steeple—
His tomb states the date it occurred.
              —anon

170

A jolly young fellow from Perth,
Was born on the day of his birth;
   He was married, they say.
   On his wife's wedding day,
And died when he quitted the earth.

—anon

171

An elderly bride of Port Jervis
Was quite understandably nervous,
   Since her apple-cheeked groom,
   With three wives in the tomb,
Kept *insuring* her during the servis.

—Ogden Nash

172

Said a cheerful young man from Torquay,
"This is rather a red-letter day;
   "I've poisoned with sherbet
   "My rich Uncle Herbert
"Whose health had not begun to decay."

—anon*

173

A poet with an M.D. diploma
Favored words with a pleasant aroma.
 When pressed for an answer,
 He never said, "cancer!"
Instead, "You have a cute carcinoma."
 —Laurence Perrine

174

With patient and loving good will
The nurses their duties fulfill!
 They wake you from sleep,
 No matter how deep,
To take your prescribed *sleeping* pill.
 —Laurence Perrine*

175

The natives got ready to serve
A midget explorer named Merve;
 "This meal will be brief,"
 Said the cannibal chief,
"For this is at best an *hors d'oeuvre*."
 —Ed Cunningham

176

There was an old Scot named McTavish,
Who attempted an anthropoid ravish,
  The object of rape
  Was the wrong sex of ape,
And the anthropoid ravished McTavish.

—anon

177

Slim Jim who's no longer a youth
Is down to his very last tooth.
  And since he can't eat
  Any red-blooded meat
He subsists on gin and vermouth.

—Lyn Nofziger*

CELEBRITIES

"Your Honor, it would be a hardship for me to sit on a long, non-celebrity trial."
—New Yorker, April 4, 2005

178

There's a notable family named Stein:
There's Gert and there's Ep and there's Ein.
   Gert's poems are bunk,
   Ep's statues are junk,
And no one can understand Ein.

          —anon

179

I sat next to the Duchess at tea.
It was just as I feared it would be
   Her rumblings abdominal
   Were simply phenomenal
And everyone thought it was me.

          —*Punch*

180

They say that ex-President Taft,
When hit by a golf ball, once laughed
   "I'm really not sore,
   "Although he called 'Fore'
"The place where he hit me was aft."

          —anon*

181

If you're looking for Albert Camus,
You should know he's not found in a zoo,
    Or a school or a church
    So pursue your research
In a library with a *Who's Who.*

                —J. Maynard Kaplan

182

A society climber from Crewe
Inquired, "What on earth will I do?
    "I of course know What's What.
    "But I fear I have not
"The faintest idea of Who's Who."

                —anon

183

A bright pert college student named Breeze,
Bogged down by BA's and BD's
    Collapsed from the strain.
    Said her doctor, "It's plain,
"You are killing yourself by degrees!"

                —anon*

MAN AND BEAST

"Yes, yes, yes, I miss you, too, honey. Now put the dog on."
—New Yorker, Aug. 22, 2005

184

Said the Reverend Henry Ward Beecher
"The hen is an elegant creature."
   The hen pleased with that
   Laid an egg in his hat.
And thus did the hen reward Beecher.
             —Oliver Wendell Holmes

185

The bustard's an exquisite fowl
With minimal reason to growl:
   He escapes what would be
   Illegitimacy
By the grace of a fortunate vowel.
             —George Vaill

186

A rare old bird is the pelican,
His bill holds more than his belican.
   He can take in his beak
   Food enough for a week:
I'm darned if I know how the helican!
             —Dixon Merritt

187

A rhinoceros rushing at Lorne
Made him wish he had never been born.
   But Lorne held his ground
   With his reason profound:
A dilemma with only one horn.

              —Albin Chaplin

188

A cheerful old bear at the Zoo
Could always find something to do.
   When it bored him, you know,
   To walk to and fro,
He reversed and walked fro and to

              —anon

189

A cat in despondency sighed,
And resolved to commit suicide;
   She passed under the wheels
   Of eight automobiles
And after the ninth one she died.

              —anon

190

"We monkeys look out for each other,"
One dandy remarked to another;
 "No creed hold I deeper
 "Than 'I'm my brother's keeper,'
"But I'm damned if I'm *my keepers brother!*"
   —Laurence Perrine

191

The cuckoo, all bird scholars attest,
Lays her eggs in another bird's nest,
 She's not really crazy.
 Just terribly lazy,
Thinks surrogate motherhood best.
   —Laurence Perrine

192

A puppy whose hair was so flowing
There really was no way of knowing
 Which end was his head,
 Once stopped me and said,
"Please, sir, am I coming or going?"
   —Oliver Herford

193

A jolly young fellow from Yuma
Told an elephant joke to a puma:
   Now his skeleton lies
   Beneath hot western skies—
The puma had no sense of huma.

                —Ogden Nash

194

My wife and I strolling one day
In the woods met a bear at play,
   He was friendly and sunny
   Till I called my wife "Honey."—
Oh, that was the wrong thing to say!

                —Laurence Perrine

195

A nice young man from the city.
Met what he thought was a kitty;
   He gave it a pat,
   Said "Nice little cat!"
They burned his clothes out of pity.

                —anon

196

You will find on the banks of the Nile
The haunts of the great crocodile.
   He will welcome you in
   With a beguiling grin
That gives way to a satisfied smile.

—anon*

197

A German explorer named Herr Schlicter
Had a yen for a boa constrictor.
   When he lifted its tail,
   Achtung! It was a male.
The constrictor, not Schlicter, was victor.

—anon

198

There was a young maid from Madras,
Who had a magnificent ass.
   It was not round and pink
   As you probably think—
It was gray, had long ears, and ate grass.

—anon

199

The three little owls in the wood,
Who always sang hymns when they could.
   What the words were about
   We could never make out,
But felt it was doing them good.

—anon

200

Said a dreadfully literate cat:
"I've had my Litt.D. and all that,
   "And in New York, my dear,
   "When I see 'Litter Here,'"
"Why I litter at once, and then scat."

—Conrad Aiken

201

A smiling young lady of Niger,
Once went for a ride on a tiger;
   They returned from the ride
   With the lady inside,
And the smile on the face of the tiger.

—anon

202

There once was a young girl who said: "How
"Can a spider, goose, and a cow
    "Have equal delights
    "And all the same rights,
"Without civil war, or a row?"

                                  —anon*

203

A careless explorer named Blake
Fell into a tropical lake.
    Said a fat alligator,
    A few minutes later:
"Very nice, but I still prefer cake."

                              —Ogden Nash

204

There was a young lady of Ryde
Who was swept far out by the tide;
    Said a man-eating shark:
    "How's this for a lark?
"I knew that the Lord would provide."

                                  —anon*

205

y young fellow name Fisher
  was fishing for fish in a fissure
  Then a cod, with a grin,
  Pulled the fisherman in . . .
Now they're searching the fissure for Fisher.

—anon

206

Said a herring one day to a sole:
"Life is very unfair—'pon my shoal!
  "While I'm stuck on a slab
  "You'll be filled with crab,
"And featured at the Ritz-Metropole."

—Stanley J. Sharpless*

SHEER NONSENSE

There was an Old Man on some rocks . . .
—Edward Lear, A Book of Nonsense, 1846

207

Recalling the limericks of Lear
We are often tempted to sneer,
    We should never forget
    That we owe him a debt
For he was the true pioneer.

—anon*

208

There was an Old Man on some rocks,
Who shut his wife in a box,
    When she said, "Let me out,"
    He exclaimed, "Without doubt,
"You will pass all your life in that box."

—Edward Lear

209

There was an old man of St. Eves
Who was stung in the head by a wasp.
    When they asked: "Does it hurt?"
    He replied: "No, it doesn't,
"I'm glad it wasn't a hornet."

—W. S. Gilbert

210

There was an Old Man who said, "How
Can I flee from this horrible Cow?
   I will sit on this stile
   And continue to smile
Which may soften the heart of the Cow."
—Edward Lear

211

There was a young man from Darjeeling.
Who got on a bus bound for Ealing;
   It said at the door:
   "Don't spit on the floor."
So he carefully spat on the ceiling.
—anon

212

There was an old man of Calcutta
Who coated his tonsils with butta,
   Thus converting his snore
   From a thunderous roar
To a soft oleaginous mutta.
—Ogden Nash

213

There was a young lady of Kent,
Whose nose was most awfully bent.
   One day, I suppose,
   She followed her nose,
For no one knew which way she went.

—anon

214

A young classical scholar from Flint
Developed a most curious squint.
   With her left-handed eye
   She could scan the whole sky
While the other was reading small print.

—anon

215

There was a young lady of Wheeling
Who had an unusual feeling,
   That she was a fly,
   And wanted to try
To walk upside down on the ceiling.

—anon

216

There was an old geezer from France
Who always wore sheet iron pants.
   He said, "Some years back
   "I sat on a tack.
"I'll never again take a chance."
—Herbert Lefever

217

A bugler named Dougal MacDougal
Found ingenious ways to be frugal.
   He learned how to Sneeze
   In various keys,
Thus saving the cost of a bugle.
—Odgen Nash

218

There was a young girl of old Natchez,
Whose garments were always in patchez;
   When comment arose
   On the state of her clothes,
She drawled: "Where Ah itchez, Ah scratchez."
—Ogden Nash

219

There was a young woman in Grinnich
Who had a great weakness for spinach.
    When it slipt down her chin
    She would lap it all in,
Initch by intich by intich.

—anon

220

There was an Old Man with a beard,
Who said: "It is just as I feared!
    "Two Owls and a Hen
    "Four Larks and a Wren,
"Have all built their nests in my beard"

—Edward Lear

221

A skeleton once in Khartoum
Invited a ghost to his room.
    They spent the whole night
    In the eeriest fight
Over who should be frightened of whom.

—anon

222

There was an old fellow of Tyre,
Who casually sat on a fire.
　　When asked, "Is it hot?"
　　He replied, "No it's not;
"I'm James Winterbottom, Esquire."

—anon

223

An accident really uncanny
Occurred to my elderly Granny;
　　She sat down in a chair
　　While her false teeth were there,
And bit herself right in the fanny.

—anon

224

A fly and a flea in a flue
Were imprisoned, so what could they do?
　　Said the fly, "Let us flee!"
　　"Let us fly!" said the flea.
So they flew through a flaw in the flue.

—anon

225

There was once a man from Nantucket
Who kept all his cash in a bucket,
    But his daughter, named Nan,
    Ran away with a man,
And as for the bucket, Nantucket.

—Dayton Voorhees

226

There was an old man of the Cape
Who made himself garments of crepe.
    When asked, "Do they tear?"
    He replied, "Here and There:
"But they're perfectly splendid for shape."

—Robert Louis Stevenson

227

Its a favorite project of mine
A new value of *pi* to assign.
    I would fix it a 3
    For it's simpler, you see,
Than 3 point 1-4-1-5-9.

—Harvey L. Carter

228

A Turk by the name of Haroun
Took whiskey by means of a spoon.
   To one who asked why,
   This Turk made reply:
"To drink is forbidden, you loon."

                  —anon

229

A father once said to his son,
"The Next time you make a bad pun,
   "Go out in the yard
   "And kick yourself hard,
"And I'll begin when you're done."

                  —anon

230

There was an Old Man of Coblenz,
The Length of whose legs was immense;
   He went with one prance,
   From Turkey to France,
That Surprising Old Man of Coblenz.

                —Edward Lear

SOURCES AND CREDITS

In assembling this highly selective collection of limericks, I have consulted more than 20 books and a number fugitive sources. I am especially indebted to authors published in the following titles: Asimov, Issac, and John Ciardi. *Limericks*. Gramercy Books, 1981; Baring-Gould, William S. *The Lure of the Limerick: An Uninhibited History*, Clarkson N. Potter, 1967; Beileson, Nick, compiler. *World's Best Limericks*. Peter Pauper Press, 1994; Duplantier, F. R. *Politickles: Limericks Lampooning the Lunatic Left*. F. R., Merrill Press, 2000.

Also: Jackson, Holbrook, editor. *The Complete Nonsense of Edward Lear*. Dover Publications, 1951; Kaplan, J. Maynard. *New Millennium Limericks for Grandmothers and Others*, Dorrance Publishing Co., 2001; Legman, G., editor. *The Limerick: 1700 Examples, With Notes, Variants, and Index*. Bell Publishing Co., MCMLXIX; Livingston, Myra Cohn, editor. *Lots of Limericks*, Margaret K. McElderry Books, 1991; Marsh, Linda, editor. *Limericks for All Occasions*. Welcome Rain Publishers, 1999, 450 pages; Parrott, E. O., editor. *The Penguin Book of Limericks*, Penguin Books, 1984.

Also: Perrine, Laurence. *A Limerick's Always A Verse: 200 Original Limericks*. Harcourt Brace Jovanovich; *Peter*

Pauper's Limerick Book, Peter Pauper Press, 1954; Reed, Langford, editor. *The Complete Limerick Book*, G. P. Putnam's Sons; Rosenbloom, Joseph, editor. *The Looniest Limerick Book in the World*, Sterling Publishing Company, 1984; Smith, Vasser W., editor. *Into the Limerick Grove: 150 Original Limericks by Contemporary Authors.* Zapizdat Publications; Staples, Rob L. *The Church Out On a Limerick*, Beacon Hill Press, 2000.

Though most of the limericks in the present volume are not copyrighted, I went to great effort to get permission from the authors and publishers I could locate. Among those whose limericks I have explicit permission to reprint are Shila Anne Barry, F. R. Duplantier, Anthony Euwer, Oliver Herford, Cosmo Monkhouse, and Lyn Nofziger. *The Penguin Book of Limericks* edited by E. O. Parrott gave permission to include verses by Frank Richards, Rod Rubin, and Stanley Sharpless.

The fifteen *New Yorker* cartoons in this volume are reproduced with the permission of the publisher.

INDEX OF AUTHORS

Of the 230 limericks in this volume, approximately 100 are anonymous. The other 130 were written by 50 known authors. Each verse falls under one of the 16 subject categories listed on the Contents page, and each is identified by its number from one to 230. Of these, ten were written by well known authors and 14 were not previously published. In every case the name of the known writer is noted after each verse. Limericks slightly modified by the editor for meter or clarity are indicated by an asterisk (*) Below is the list of known authors and the number of the verse or verses by each included in this collection.

Aiken, Conrad, 200
Auden, W. H., 91

Barry, Sheila Anne, 94
Best, C. F., 125
Braley, Berton, 114
Buller, A. H. R., 124

Carter, Harvey L., 227
Cass, Stephen, 162
Catley, Douglas, 75

Chaplain, Albin, 187
Ciardi, John, 15, 19, 131, 157, 158, 160
Cinna, A., 87
Cunningham, Ed, 175

Duplantier, F.R., 68, 79, 80, 81, 82, 98, 121, 138, 139, 140, 142

Field, Eugene, 133

Gilbert, W. S., 64, 209
Gray, Victor, 161

Hanney, G. W., 5
Hare, M. E., 52
Herford, Oliver, 192
Holmes, Oliver Wendell, 41, 184

Johnson, Joyce, 119

Kaplan, J. Maynard, 96, 167, 181
Knox, Ronald, 48

Lear, Edward, 20, 208, 210, 220, 230
Lefever, Ernest W., 39, 51, 55, 65, 77, 116, 129, 132, 152
Lefever, Herbert, 216
Lubovich, Anatole T., 90

Merritt, Dixon, 186
Monkhouse, Cosmo, 2

Nash, Ogden, 1, 23, 85, 89, 171, 193, 203, 212, 217, 218
Nofziger, Lyn, 31, 57, 84, 177

Parr, Joyce, 70
Perrine, Laurence, 3, 16, 21, 42, 43, 69, 83, 100, 105, 113, 118, 120, 122, 141, 151, 154, 164, 168, 173, 174, 190, 191, 194
Price, W. H. G., 67

Richards, Frank, 71, 88, 103, 153
Rosenbloom, Joseph, 146
Rubin, Ron, 107
Russell, Bertrand, 166

Sharpless, Stanley, 102, 115, 206
Smith, Vasser W., 117
Staples, Rob L., 44, 45, 53, 74
Stevenson, Robert Louis, 226

Temple, William, 46
Thorneley, Thomas, 99, 104

Vaill, George, 185
Voorhees, Dayton, 225

Watson, Frank, 62
Webster, A. W., 72
Wells, Carolyn, 108
Wilkins, A. N., 73

ABOUT THE AUTHOR

In addition to Ernest Lefever's lifelong fascination with the limerick, duly noted in the introduction, he has had time for other pursuits. He is a senior fellow at the Ethics and Public Policy Center in Washington, a think tank he founded in 1976 to "clarify and reinforce the bond between the Judeo-Christian moral tradition and domestic and foreign policy issues." He received a B.D. and Ph.D. in Christian Ethics from Yale University.

He has been a senior researcher at the Johns Hopkins School of Advanced International Studies, the Brookings Institution, the Congressional Research Service of the Library of Congress, and the Institute for Defense Analyses, all located in Washington, D.C.

Dr. Lefever spent three years in Britain and West Germany after World war II (1945–1948) as a field secretary of the World's Alliance of YMCAs, working among returning German prisoners of war.

In addition to his first book, *Ethics and United States Foreign Policy* (1957), he has written *Crisis in the Congo* (1965), *TV and National Defense* (1974), *Nuclear Arms in the Third World* (1979), *Amsterdam to Nairobi: The World Council of Churches and the Third World* (1979), *The Irony of Virtue* (1998), and *America's Imperial Burden* (1999).